Back to School with New Friends

Written by
J.P Anthony Williams

In a cozy corner of Whispering Woods, the first day of school had arrived.

Bella the Bunny was excited but nervous at the same time.

When Bella arrived at the Forest School, she was greeted by Miss Honeydew the Bear, who was warm and welcoming.

Miss Honeydew: "Welcome, Bella! We're so happy to have you here. Let me introduce you to some of your classmates."

Bella looked around the bright, cheerful classroom filled with colorful drawings and cozy reading nooks.
She felt a little overwhelmed until Max the Fox trotted up to her with a friendly smile.

As the day went on, Bella participated in various activities but still felt a little homesick. During art class, she drew a picture of her home with her mom, which made her feel better.

Oliver the Owl noticed Bella's drawing and flew over.
Oliver: "That's a lovely picture, Bella. Would you like to join our art club? We can draw together every week."
Bella: "I'd love to, Oliver. Thank you!"

At lunchtime, Bella sat alone for a bit, missing her mom. Lily the Squirrel saw her and decided to join her.

Lily: "Hey, Bella! My friends and I are playing a game after lunch. Want to join us?"

Bella: "What game are you playing?"

After lunch, Bella, Max, Oliver, and Lily played hide and seek together. They laughed and explored, finding the best hiding spots behind trees and bushes.

As the school day came to an end, Bella felt much happier. She realized she had made wonderful new friends who made her feel welcome and included.

Bella hugged her new friends and waved goodbye to Miss Honeydew.
Bella: "See you all tomorrow!"

As Bella hopped home, she couldn't wait to tell her mom about her exciting first day at Forest School and all the new friends she had made.

The forest echoed with the sounds of happy animals, and Bella knew that no matter what, she would always have fun and supportive friends by her side.

THE END

Scan QR code to check out the other books in this series

SCAN ME

Thank You- <u>Free</u> Gift

Thank you for reading "Back to School with New Friends"
I hope you enjoyed it and if you have a minute to spare, I would be extremely grateful if you could post <u>a short review on my book's Amazon page.</u>

To show my gratitude, I am offering a FREE copy of the <u>Animals Coloring Book for children.</u> Download your free copy by scanning this QR code with your phone camera

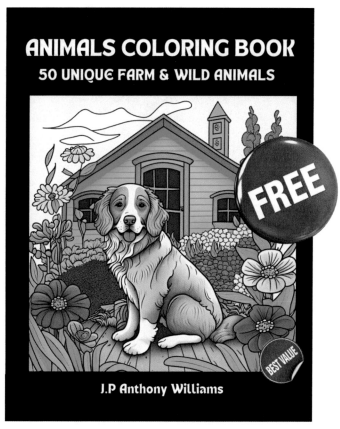

What's Next

Scan the QR code to check out the other books in this Series

SCAN ME

What's Next

Scan the QR code to check out the other books in this Series

What's Next

Scan the QR code to check out the other books in this Series

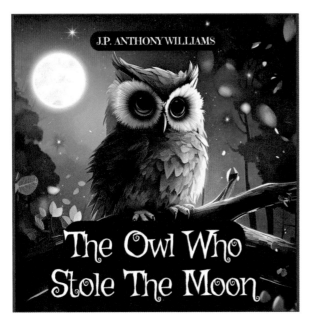

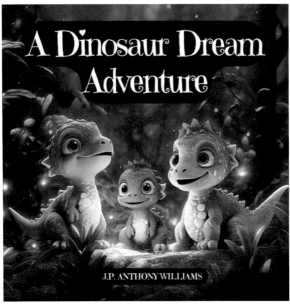

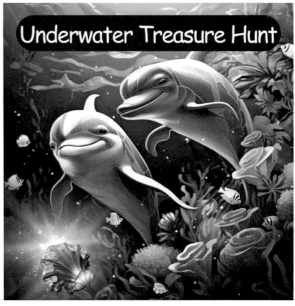

What's Next

Scan the QR code to check out the other books in this Series

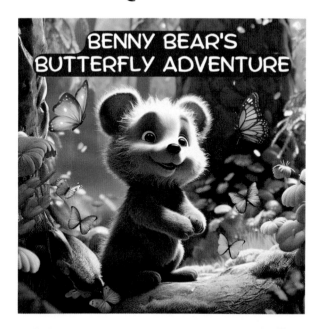

The world of
J.P. Anthony Williams

About the Author

J.P Anthony Williams is a bestselling children's book author, known for his enchanting tales and vivid illustrations. His stories are loved by young readers all over the world.

Born and raised in a small town, J.P developed a love of nature and storytelling at an early age. He spent his childhood exploring the woods and fields near his home, and he loved nothing more than curling up with a good book.

J.P's stories are known for their vivid imagery and richly-detailed illustrations. He takes inspiration from the natural world and from the myths and legends of his childhood, and he weaves them into tales that are both entertaining and educational.

In his free time, J.P can be found exploring new places and seeking inspiration for his next book. He is also a big advocate for environmental conservation, and often uses his platform to raise awareness about nature and its preservation.